FOREWORD

The WORKBOOK FOR STRINGS, Books I and II, stress the names of notes, finger patterns, scales, key signatures, terms and symbols, and other information necessary to prepare the string player thoroughly for orchestra membership.

Book I, 44 pages, covers the problems encountered during the first year or so of string study.

Book II, 40 pages, briefly reviews the Book I material, covers all keys, finger patterns, string terms, signs and symbols, and corresponds to material found in most second and third year method books.

Published in separate books for each of the stringed instruments, the material is in workbook form so that the assignments can be completed at home to save rehearsal time. Only a minimum amount of classroom explanation is necessary.

Book I	Book II
Violin	Violin
Viola	Viola
Cello	Cello
Bass	Bass

Forest R. Etling

WORKBOOK FOR STRINGS
BOOK 1

Student Record   Name _____

Page	Assigned (√)	Grade	Page	Assigned (√)	Grade
1			23		
2			24		
3			25		
4			26		
5			27		
6			28		
7			29		
8			30		
9			31		
10			32		
11			33		
12			34		
13			35		
14			36		
15			37		
16			38		
17			39		
18			40		
19			41		
20			42		
21			43		
22			44		

IMPORTANT INFORMATION

1. Each violinist and violist should have a fully equipped, well-adjusted outfit with adjustable pad, string adjusters, and cake of inexpensive but good rosin. Cello and bass players should also be comparably well-equipped.

2. Each student should practice at least 30 minutes daily.

3. Each student should have an adjustable music stand.

4. The violin and bow should be kept in the case when not in use.

5. The fingers should not touch the bow hair.

6. Loosen the bow hair after playing...just enough to take the tension off of the stick.

7. To play, tighten the hair enough to have clearance for the width of a pencil.

8. The bow must be rosined for every practice session.

9. Wipe the rosin dust from the instrument and strings with a soft cloth daily. Carry a 12" X 12" cleaning cloth in the case at all times.

10. Keep the instrument away from heat, radiators, excessively hot sun, excessive cold or quick changes in temperature.

11. When repairs are needed, have your teacher suggest a qualified repairman.

12. A new violin outfit is generally much better than an old outfit. However, good adjustment... such as properly fitted pegs and a well-fitted bridge...are most important for all instruments.

13. There are about 70 parts to the violin.

14. The top is spruce while the back is maple.

15. The black ebony wood comes from Africa.

16. The pernambuco wood of the bow comes from South America.

17. The bow hair comes from Siberia.

18. The violin form was perfected in Italy.

19. The bow hair has many small teeth that bite into the string, while the rosin catches and clings to the string.

20. The violin is the "king" of all instruments, while the string section is the most important section of the orchestra.

TEST

1. The string section is the most important section of the _____ .

2. Each student should practice _____ minutes daily.

3. Each student should have an adjustable music _____ .

4. The violin and bow should be kept in the _____ when not in use.

5. The _____ must not touch the bow hair.

6. The hair should be _____ after playing.

7. The bow should be rosined for _____ practice session.

8. The instrument should be kept away from small children and _____ .

9. The bow hair usually comes from _____ .

10. The black _____ wood comes from Africa.

11. The pernambuco wood comes from _____ .

12. The form of the violin was perfected in _____ .

13. The top of the violin is made of spruce, while the back is _____ .

14. There are approximately _____ parts to the violin.

15. Bow hair has many small _____ that bite into the string.

16. A _____ violin is generally better than an old violin.

17. When repairs are needed, have your _____ suggest a repairman.

18. The rosin dust should be wiped away daily with a _____ .

19. Each student should have a cake of inexpensive but good _____ .

20. The bow hair should be tightened just enough to have tension on the hair and stick, or so that there is a clearance for the width of a _____ between the hair and stick at the middle of the bow.

THE INSTRUMENT AND BOW

DIRECTIONS:

Learn the parts of the instrument and bow.

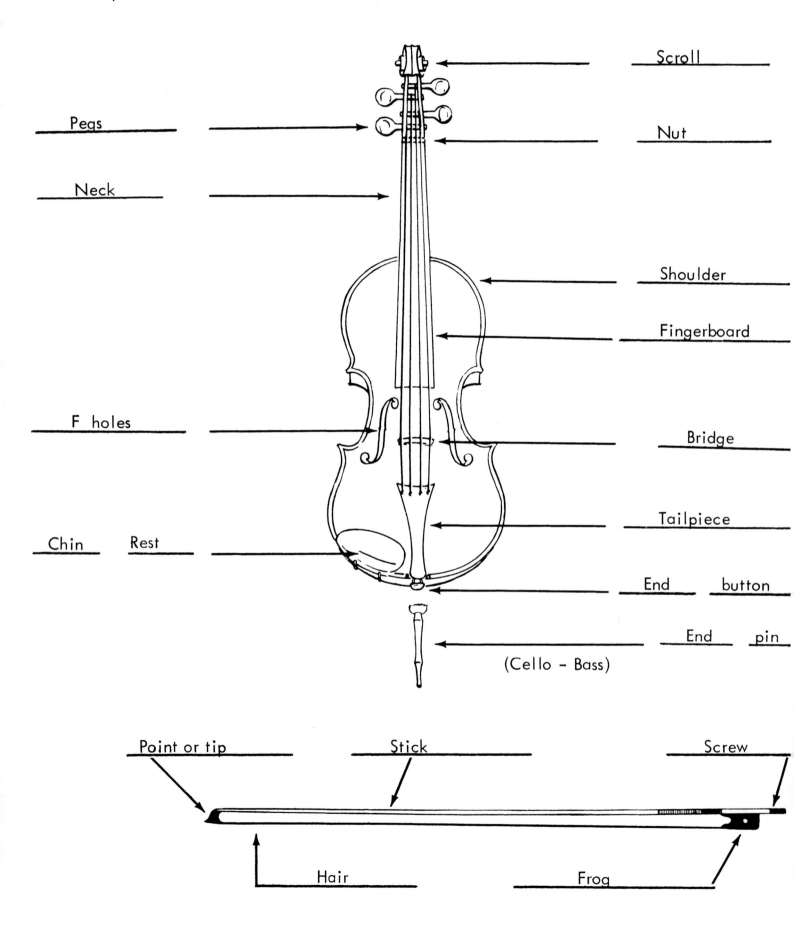

Scroll

Peas

Nut

Neck

Shoulder

Fingerboard

F holes

Bridge

Tailpiece

Chin   Rest

End   button

End   pin

(Cello - Bass)

Point or tip   Stick   Screw

Hair   Frog

THE INSTRUMENT AND BOW TEST

DIRECTIONS:

Name the parts of the instrument and bow.

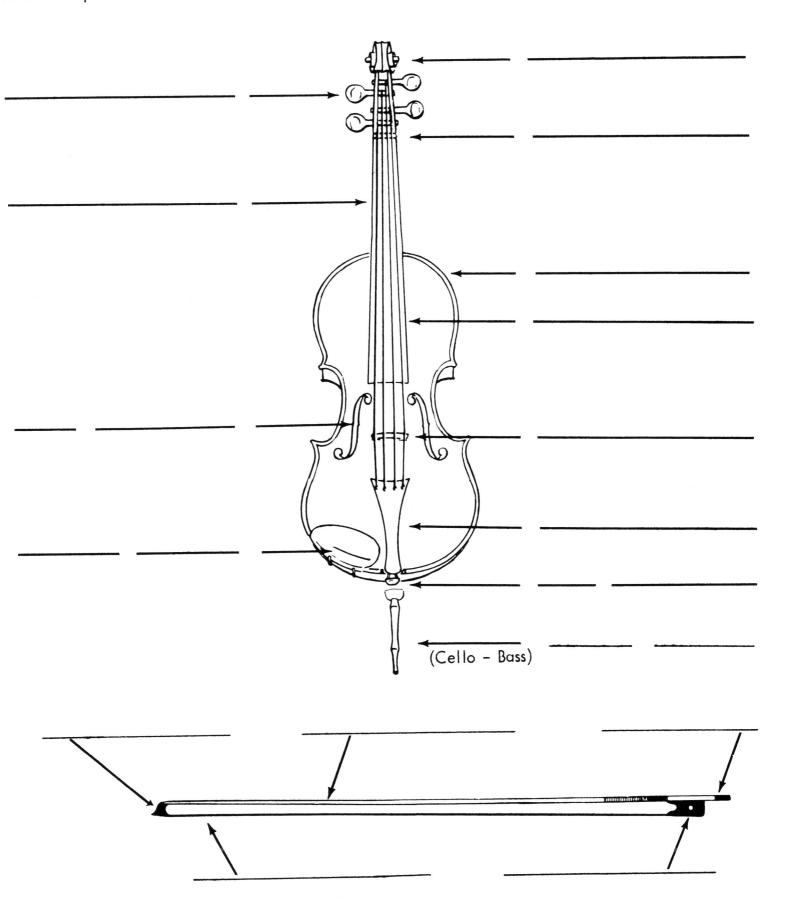

(Cello - Bass)

PEGS

CELLO PEGS

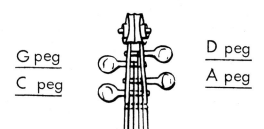

G peg

C peg

D peg

A peg

DIRECTIONS:

Name each PEG.
Fill in the blanks.

CELLO PEGS

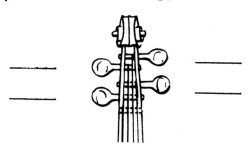

—— ——

—— ——

DIRECTIONS:

Cello players, practice drawing some bass clef signs.

OPEN STRINGS AND THEIR NAMES

C G D A

DIRECTIONS:

Write the letter name under each note of the open strings.

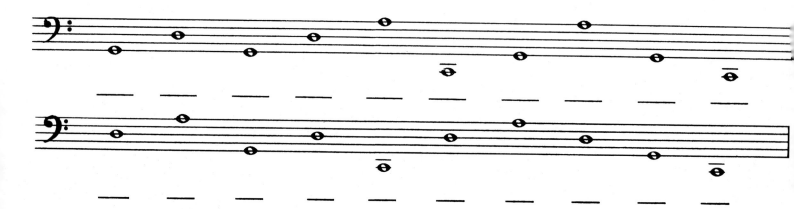

NOTES AND THEIR NAMES

The STAFF is a combination of the treble and bass clef staffs, as commonly seen in piano music, which in reality is one large staff. Middle C, as shown below, is located at the mid point between both staffs.

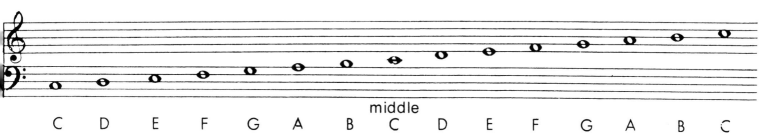

C   D   E   F   G   A   B   middle C   D   E   F   G   A   B   C

LETTER NAMES OF THE SPACES
For the Bass Clef:

A   C   E   G

For the names of notes located on spaces in the Bass Clef, memorize:

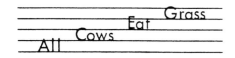

LETTER NAMES OF THE LINES
For the Bass Clef:

G   B   D   F   A

An easy method for learning the names of notes occurring on the lines in the Bass Clef is to memorize:

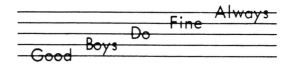

LINES AND SPACES ABOVE AND BELOW THE STAFF

Usually music requires the use of tones higher or lower than the staff can accommodate. Through the use of ledger lines, the staff may be extended above and below.

BASS CLEF:

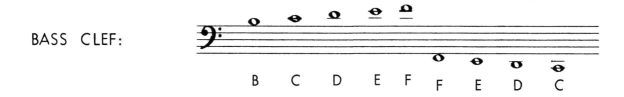

B   C   D   E   F   F   E   D   C

DIRECTIONS: Write the letter name of each of the following notes.

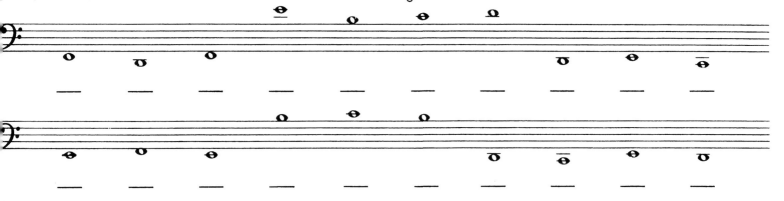

DRAWING WHOLE NOTES

DIRECTIONS:

Place the appropriate clef sign on the staffs below and draw the proper note above the letter name

(Notes: ⌒ + ⌣ = 𝗢)

G   D   C   B   A   E   F   B   E   C

C   E   G   B   D   F   A   C   E   G

A   C   E   G   B   D   F   A   C   E

G   C   F   B   E   A   D   G   C   F

D   F   E   G   F   A   G   B   A   C

A   C   E   G   B   D   F   A   C   F

C   A   G   B   D   F   A   C   E   F

A   C   E   B   A   D   B   E   G   E

DRAWING QUARTER NOTES

DIRECTIONS:

Place the appropriate clef sign on the staffs below and draw the proper note above the letter names

1. All single notes located above the third line on the staff will have the stem drawn down from the left side of the note head.

2. All single notes located on or below the third line of the staff will have the stem drawn up from the right side of the note head.

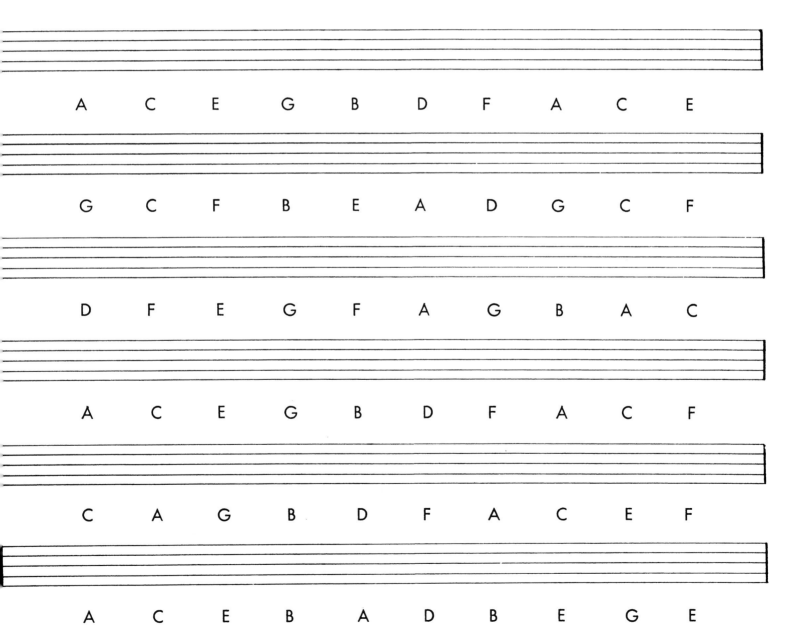

MUSICAL SPELLING BEE

DIRECTIONS:

Draw the clef sign for your instrument.

Draw the notes to spell the following words on the staff.

Treble Clef Example:

E G G

Viola Clef Example:

E G G

Bass Clef Example:

E G G

1. ace
2. egg
3. be
4. fad
5. bag
6. gag
7. age
8. cab
9. gab
10. beg
11. bed
12. dab
13. bad
14. add
15. bee
16. fed
17. cad
18. ace
19. dead
20. cage
21. deed
22. fade
23. beef
24. feed
25. deaf
26. babe
27. bead
28. face
29. gage
30. cafe

MUSICAL SPELLING BEE

DIRECTIONS:

1. Draw the clef sign for your instrument.
2. Draw the notes that these words spell.

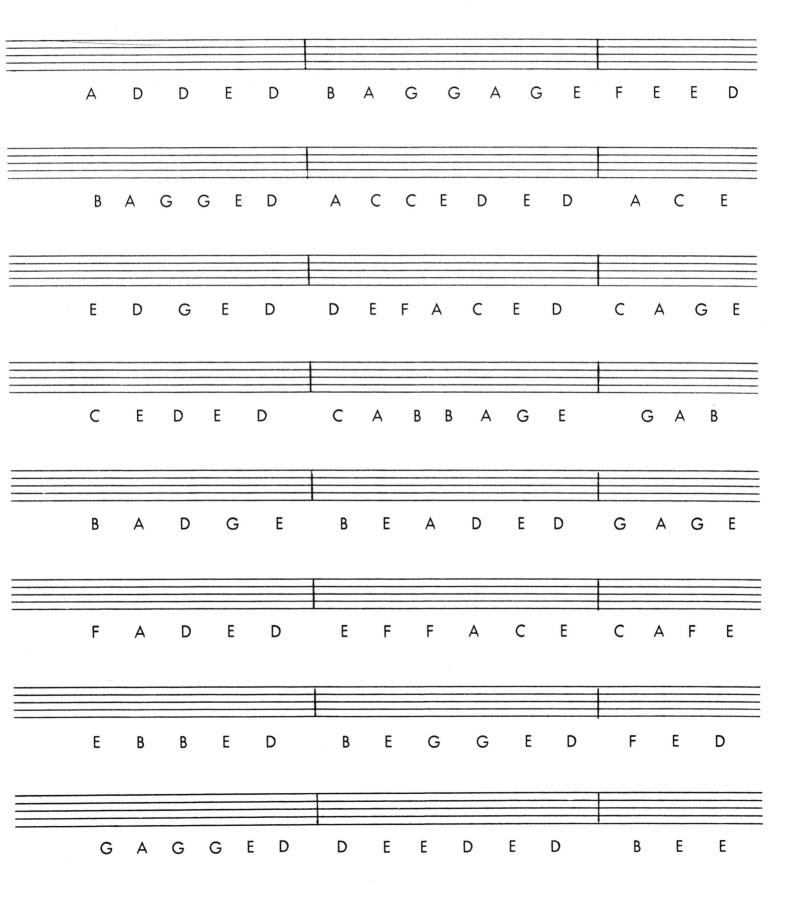

A D D E D   B A G G A G E   F E E D

B A G G E D   A C C E D E D   A C E

E D G E D   D E F A C E D   C A G E

C E D E D   C A B B A G E   G A B

B A D G E   B E A D E D   G A G E

F A D E D   E F F A C E   C A F E

E B B E D   B E G G E D   F E D

G A G G E D   D E E D E D   B E E

NOTE VALUES

The WHOLE NOTE receives 4 beats.

(1) Draw a row of whole notes. _____

The HALF NOTE receives 2 beats.

(2) Draw a row of half notes. _____

The QUARTER NOTE receives 1 beat.

(3) Draw a row of quarter notes. _____

(4)

DIRECTIONS:

Write the NUMBER OF BEATS under each note.

(5)

DIRECTIONS:

Draw "arrows" under each note according to the number of beats each note receives.

NOTE VALUE TEST

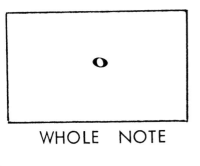

WHOLE NOTE

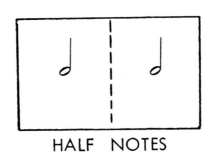

HALF NOTES

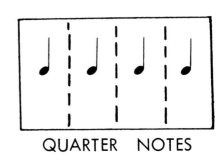

QUARTER NOTES

(1) DIRECTIONS:

Write the correct number in the blank space.

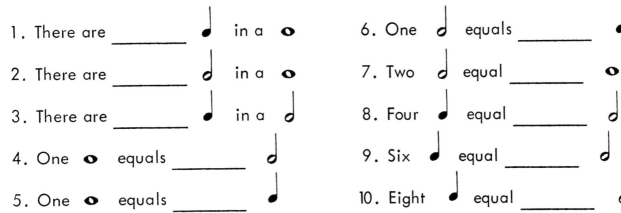

1. There are _____ ♩ in a 𝅝   6. One 𝅗𝅥 equals _____ ♩

2. There are _____ 𝅗𝅥 in a 𝅝   7. Two 𝅗𝅥 equal _____ 𝅝

3. There are _____ ♩ in a 𝅗𝅥   8. Four ♩ equal _____ 𝅗𝅥

4. One 𝅝 equals _____ 𝅗𝅥   9. Six ♩ equal _____ 𝅗𝅥

5. One 𝅝 equals _____ ♩   10. Eight ♩ equal _____ 𝅗𝅥

(2) DIRECTIONS:

Fill in the blanks with the proper answer.

1. There are _____ quarter notes in a whole note.

2. There are _____ half notes in a whole note.

3. There are _____ quarter notes in a half note.

4. There are _____ quarter notes in two half notes.

5. There are _____ quarter notes in three half notes.

6. A whole note equals _____ half notes.

7. A whole note equals _____ quarter notes.

8. A half note equals _____ quarter notes.

9. Two half notes equal _____ quarter notes.

10. Four quarter notes equal _____ whole note.

REST VALUES

The WHOLE REST receives 4 beats.

① Draw a row of whole rests. _____

The HALF REST receives 2 beats.

② Draw a row of half rests. _____

The QUARTER REST receives 1 beat.

③ Draw a row of quarter rests. _____

④ DIRECTIONS:

After each note on the staff below, draw its REST equivalent.

⑤ DIRECTIONS:

Under each NOTE or REST, write the number of beats it receives.

REST VALUE TEST

WHOLE REST HALF RESTS QUARTER RESTS

① DIRECTIONS:

Write the correct number in the blank space.

1. There are _____ 𝄽 in a 𝄻   6. One 𝄼 equals _____ 𝄽

2. There are _____ 𝄼 in a 𝄻   7. Two 𝄼 equal _____ 𝄻

3. There are _____ 𝄽 in a 𝄼   8. Four 𝄽 equal _____ 𝄼

4. One 𝄻 equals _____ 𝄼   9. Six 𝄽 equal _____ 𝄼

5. One 𝄻 equals _____ 𝄽   10. Eight 𝄽 equal _____ 𝄼

② DIRECTIONS:

Fill in the blanks with the proper answer.

1. There are _____ quarter rests in a whole rest.

2. There are _____ half rests in a whole rest.

3. There are _____ quarter rests in a half rest.

4. There are _____ quarter rests in two half rests.

5. There are _____ quarter rests in three half rests.

6. A whole rest equals _____ half rests.

7. A whole rest equals _____ quarter rests.

8. A half rest equals _____ quarter rests.

9. Two half rests equal _____ quarter rests.

10. Four quarter rests equal _____ whole rest.

TIME SIGNATURES

4 = The top number tells how many counts in a measure.

4 = The bottom number tells what kind of note will receive one count.

① DIRECTIONS:

Fill in the blanks.

3/4   There are _____ counts in a measure in 3/4 time.

2/4   A _____ _____ gets one count in 2/4 time.

6/8   There are _____ counts in a measure in 6/8 time.

6/8   An _____ _____ gets one count in 6/8 time.

2/2   A _____ _____ gets one count in 2/2 time.

② DIRECTIONS:

Place the correct time signature after adding the clef sign. The quarter note is the "one count" note.

EIGHTH NOTES AND RESTS

The EIGHTH NOTE receives ½ a beat.

(1) Draw a row of eighth notes. _____

Two eighth notes receive 1 beat.

(2) Draw several pairs of eighth notes. _____

The EIGHTH REST receives ½ a beat.

(3) Draw a row of eighth rests. _____

(4) DIRECTIONS:

In the following measures, count the time aloud while tapping your foot. Tap your foot "down" on the "beat" and "up" on the "and."

1 2 an 3 4 an   1 2 an 3 an 4   1 an 2 an 3 an 4   1 an 2 an 3 an 4 an

(5) DIRECTIONS:

In the following exercises, write the beats under each note and rest. Count the time aloud while tapping your foot.

DOTTED NOTES

A DOT PLACED AFTER A NOTE INCREASES THE LENGTH OF THAT NOTE ONE-HALF ITS VALUE

(1) DIRECTIONS:

Write the correct number in the blank space.

1. There are _____ 𝅘𝅥 in a 𝅝.

2. There are _____ 𝅗𝅥 in a 𝅝.

3. There are _____ 𝅘𝅥 in a 𝅗𝅥.

4. There are _____ 𝅘𝅥 + _____ 𝅗𝅥 in a 𝅝.

5. There are _____ 𝅘𝅥 + _____ 𝅗𝅥. in a 𝅝.

6. There are _____ 𝅘𝅥 + _____ 𝅗𝅥 in a 𝅝

7. One 𝅝. equals _____ 𝅗𝅥

8. One 𝅗𝅥. equals _____ 𝅘𝅥

9. One 𝅝. equals one 𝅗𝅥 and _____ 𝅘𝅥

10. One 𝅗𝅥. equals one 𝅗𝅥 and _____ 𝅘𝅥

(2) DIRECTIONS:

Write the number of the beat under each note and rest in the following measures.

TEST

Note and Rest Values:

𝅝 = 4   ♩ = 1   𝅗𝅥· = 3   𝄾 = 1

𝅗𝅥 = 2   𝅝· = 6   ▬ = 2   ▆ = 4

ADDITION

Add the values of the notes and rests.

1. 𝅝 + 𝅝 + 𝅗𝅥 + 𝅗𝅥 = _____

2. ♩ + 𝄾 + ▬ + 𝄾 = _____

3. 𝅝· + 𝅗𝅥· + 𝅗𝅥 + 𝅗𝅥· = _____

4. ▆ + ▬ + 𝅗𝅥 + ▆ = _____

5. 𝅝 + 𝄾 + ▬ + 𝅗𝅥 = _____

SUBTRACTION

Subtract the value of the second note or rest from the first note or rest.

1. 𝅝 − ♩ = _____

2. 𝅝· − ♩ = _____

3. ▆ − 𝅗𝅥· = _____

4. ▬ − 𝄾 = _____

5. ▆ − ▬ = _____

6. 𝅝· − ♩ = _____

7. 𝅝 − 𝄾 = _____

BALANCE THE SCALES

DIRECTIONS:

Put notes or rests on the <u>right</u> hand scale that will equal the value of the notes or rests on the <u>left</u> hand scale. Notes can be balanced by notes <u>or</u> rests. Rests can be balanced by rests <u>or</u> notes.

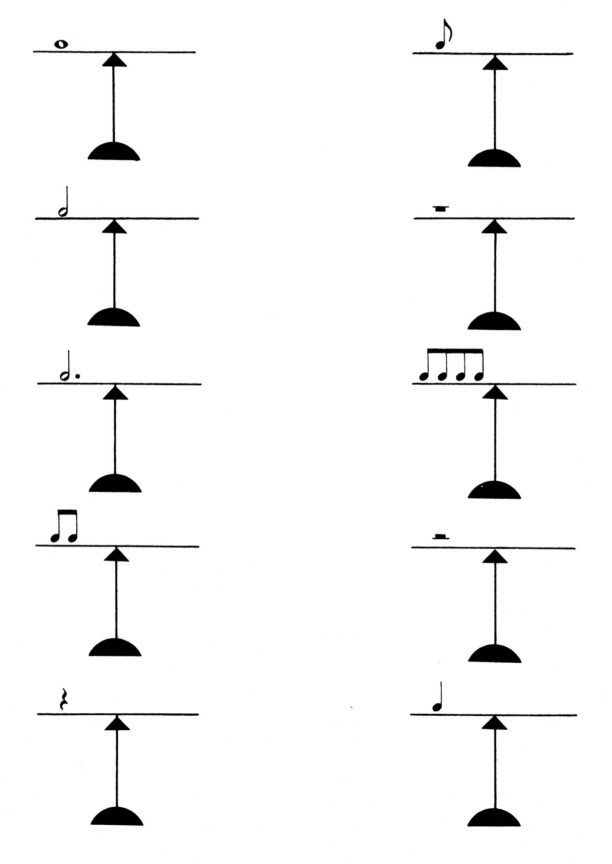

ACCIDENTAL SHARPS, FLATS, AND NATURALS

Sharps (♯) raise the sound of notes.

Flats (♭) lower the sound of notes.

Naturals (♮) cancel the effect of a sharp or flat.

Accidentals are sharps or flats placed in front of notes to raise or lower them.

The signs, ♯ , ♭ , and ♮ , are placed in front of the note (♯ ♩); but the signs are placed behind the letter name (F ♯).

① DIRECTIONS:

Draw your clef sign and write the correct name of the following notes.

② DIRECTIONS:

Draw the clef sign and the note and correct sign on the proper line or space.

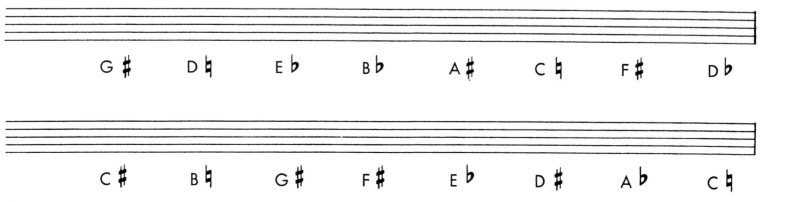

G♯   D♮   E♭   B♭   A♯   C♮   F♯   D♭

C♯   B♮   G♯   F♯   E♭   D♯   A♭   C♮

MUSIC TERMS AND SIGNS

1. Pizzicato (Pizz) = Pluck with the "pointer" finger of right hand

2. Arco = Use the bow

3. $\overset{V}{\mathbf{\cdot}|}$ = Pick-up note (note before the bar line), use up bow

4. ⌢ (Fermata) = Hold beyond the note or rest value

5. $\overset{+}{\mathbf{\cdot}}$ = Pluck with the left hand

6. Fine = The end

7. D.C. al fine = Go back to beginning and play to Fine

8. p (piano) = Soft

9. pp (pianissimo) = Very soft

10. f (forte) = Loud

11. ff (fortissimo) = Very loud

12. mp (mezzo piano) = Medium soft

13. mf (mezzo forte) = Medium loud

14. Ritard (rit) = Gradually slower

15. Legato = Smoothly

16. Moderato = Play at a medium speed

17. Andante = Play at a medium slow speed

18. Allegro = Fast, quick, lively

19. Maestoso = Play in a stately, majestic manner

20. Diminuendo (dim) (⟩) = Gradually softer

21. M. = Play at the middle of the bow

22. Pt. = Play at the point of the bow

23. Fr. = Play at the frog of the bow

24. L.H. = Use the lower half of bow

25. U.H. = Use the upper half of bow

TERMS AND SIGNS TEST

DIRECTIONS:

State what the word, abbreviation, or sign wants you to do.

1. Arco _____

2. Pizz. _____

3. Legato _____

4. Moderato _____

5. D.C. al fine _____

6. Dim. _____

7. ♩⁺ _____

8. ⌢ _____

9. M. _____

10. Pt. _____

11. L.H. _____

12. U.H. _____

13. p _____

14. Rit. _____

15. mp _____

16. pp _____

17. Fr. _____

18. ♩∨ _____

19. Andante _____

20. f _____

21. mf _____

22. ff _____

23. Allegro _____

24. Maestoso _____

25. Fine _____

TEST

DIRECTIONS:

Place the number of the correct answer in the space opposite the definition.

_____	1. played with the bow	1. f-holes
_____	2. upper number of time signature	2. rosin
_____	3. lower number of time signature	3. $\frac{1}{2}$ and whole steps
_____	4. straight line with the bridge	4. soundpost
_____	5. direction the bow-stick leans	5. bridge
_____	6. playing with correct pitch	6. ⊓
_____	7. ♩ ♩ ♩ ♩	7. slur
_____	8. ♫♫	8. lower end of bow
_____	9. music of one instrument	9. V
_____	10. playing together of several players	10. tie
_____	11. played by plucking the strings	11. upper end of bow
_____	12. part of violin under strings	12. arco
_____	13. sides of the violin	13. counts per measure
_____	14. distance between musical sounds	14. one count note
_____	15. openings in top of the instrument	15. good intonation
_____	16. conditions the bow for playing	16. to the fingerboard
_____	17. raises strings off fingerboard	17. bow stroke
_____	18. necessary for a good bow grip	18. 1 2 3 4
_____	19. inside violin, behind bridge	19. 1 & 2 &
_____	20. point or tip	20. solo
_____	21. frog or nut	21. ensemble
_____	22. up-bow (from point to frog)	22. pizzicato
_____	23. down-bow (from frog to point)	23. curved thumb
_____	24. notes of same pitch connected by a curved line	24. fingerboard
_____	25. unlike pitches played on same bow	25. ribs

NOTES ON THE D STRING

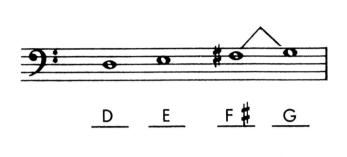

D   E   F♯   G

DIRECTIONS:

1. Write the letter names.

2. Mark the ½ steps. (∧)

(Note that the sharp is now in the key signature.)

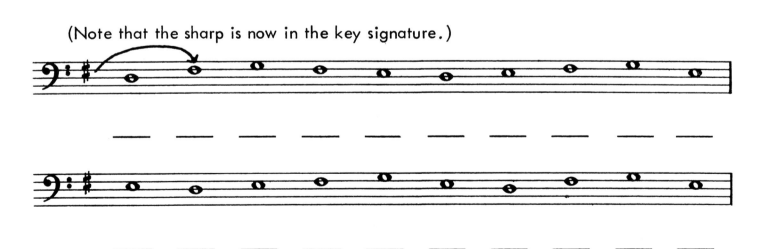

NOTES ON THE A STRING

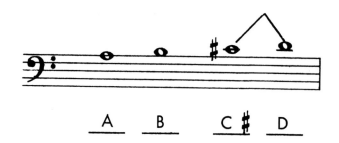

A   B   C♯   D

A

DIRECTIONS:

1. Write the letter names.

2. Mark the $\frac{1}{2}$ steps. (ʌ)

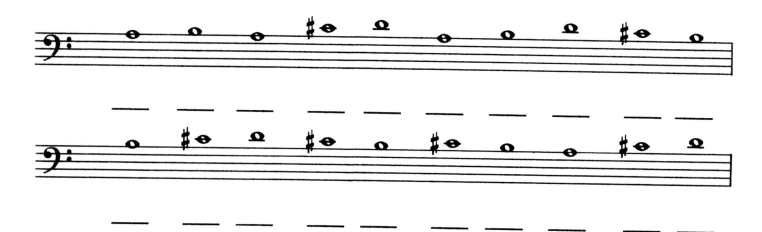

(Note that the sharp is now in the key signature.)

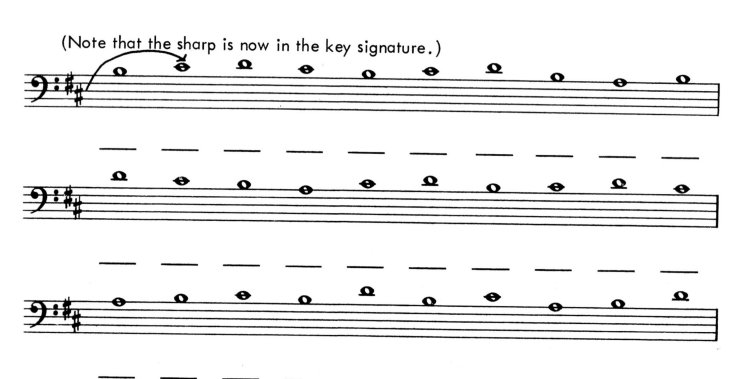

NOTES ON THE G STRING

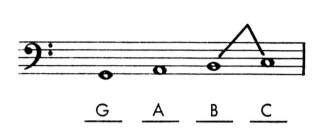

G   A   B   C

DIRECTIONS:

1. Write the letter names.

2. Mark the $\frac{1}{2}$ steps. (∧)

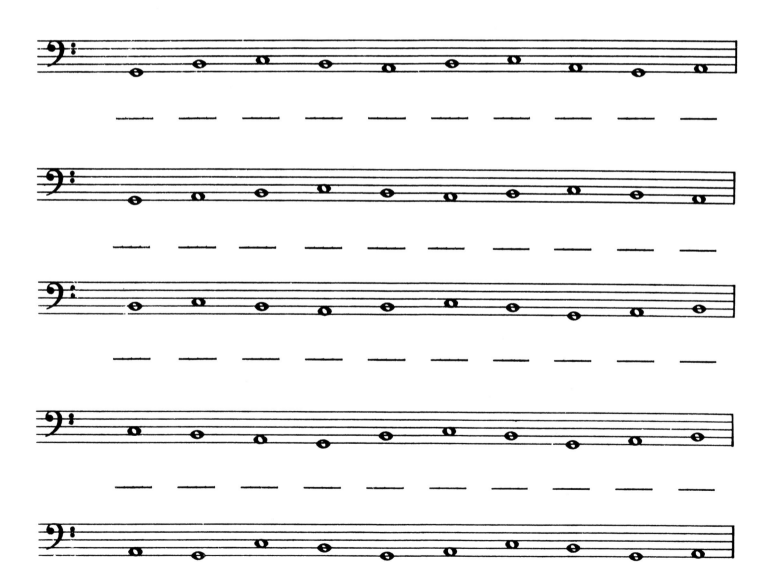

NOTES ON THE C STRING

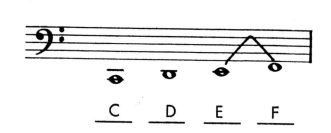

C   D   E   F

C

DIRECTIONS:

1. Write the letter names.

2. Mark the ½ steps. (∧)

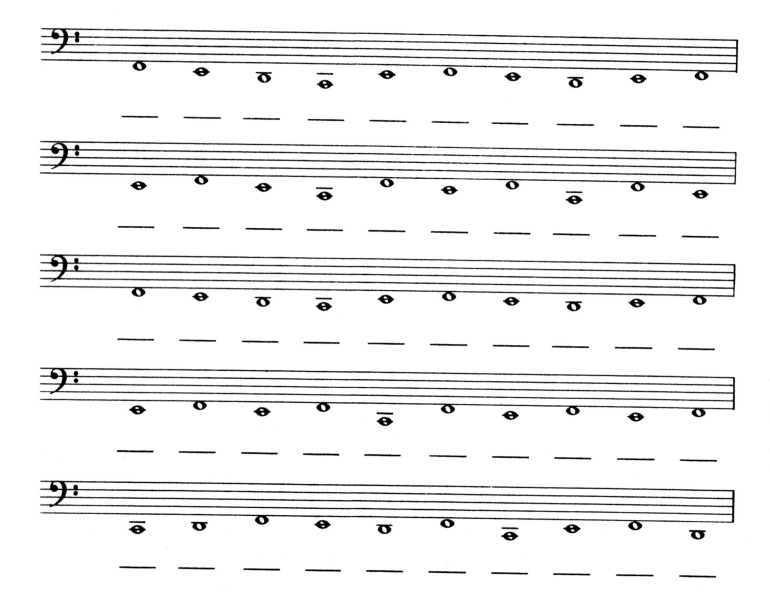

REVIEW

DIRECTIONS:

1. Name the notes. (Observe the key signature.)

2. Mark the ½ steps. (∧)

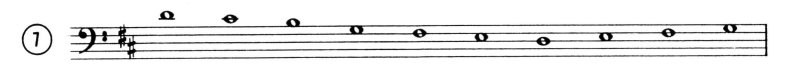

THE 3-4 PATTERN

DIRECTIONS:

1. Write the notes that occur on each string if the ½ step occurs between the 3rd and 4th fingers. (Use accidentals.)

2. Name the notes.

3. Mark the ½ steps. (∧)

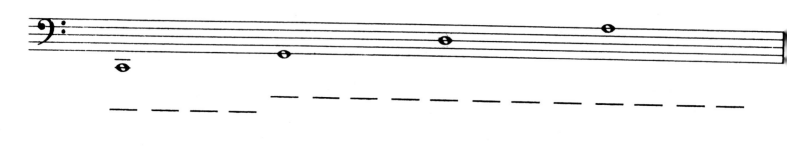

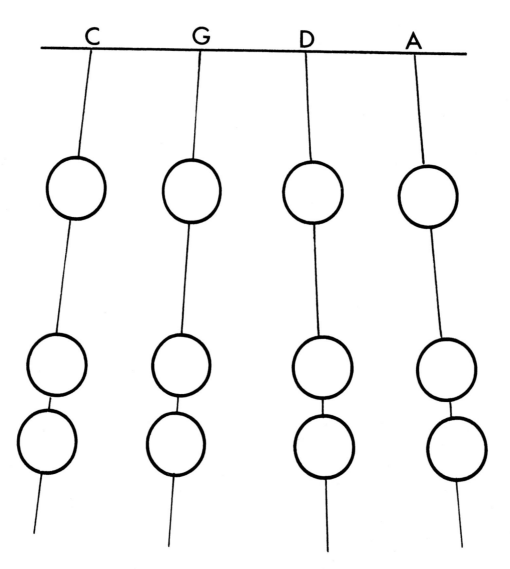

THE THIRD FINGERS

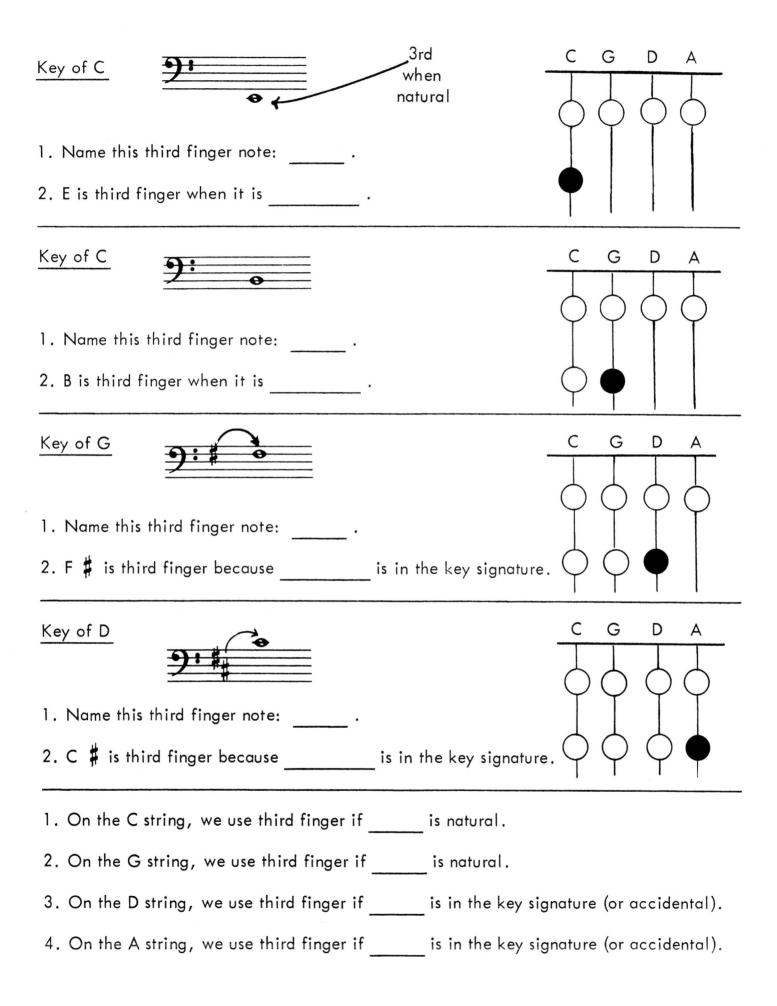

Key of C

1. Name this third finger note: _____ .

2. E is third finger when it is _____ .

Key of C

1. Name this third finger note: _____ .

2. B is third finger when it is _____ .

Key of G

1. Name this third finger note: _____ .

2. F ♯ is third finger because _____ is in the key signature.

Key of D

1. Name this third finger note: _____ .

2. C ♯ is third finger because _____ is in the key signature.

1. On the C string, we use third finger if _____ is natural.

2. On the G string, we use third finger if _____ is natural.

3. On the D string, we use third finger if _____ is in the key signature (or accidental).

4. On the A string, we use third finger if _____ is in the key signature (or accidental).

THIRD FINGERS (continued)

(1) What is necessary in the key signature to have the third finger on the C string? _____ .

Use third finger on the C when it is _____ .

(2) What is necessary in the key signature to have the third finger on the G string? _____ .

Use third finger on the G when it is _____ .

(3) What is necessary in the key signature to have the third finger on the D string? _____ .

Place that sharp in the key signature.

(4) What is necessary in the key signature to have the third finger on the A string? _____ .

Place that sharp in the key signature.

(5) Put all of the sharps in the key signature that are necessary to have all of the third fingers.

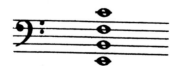

THE SECOND FINGERS

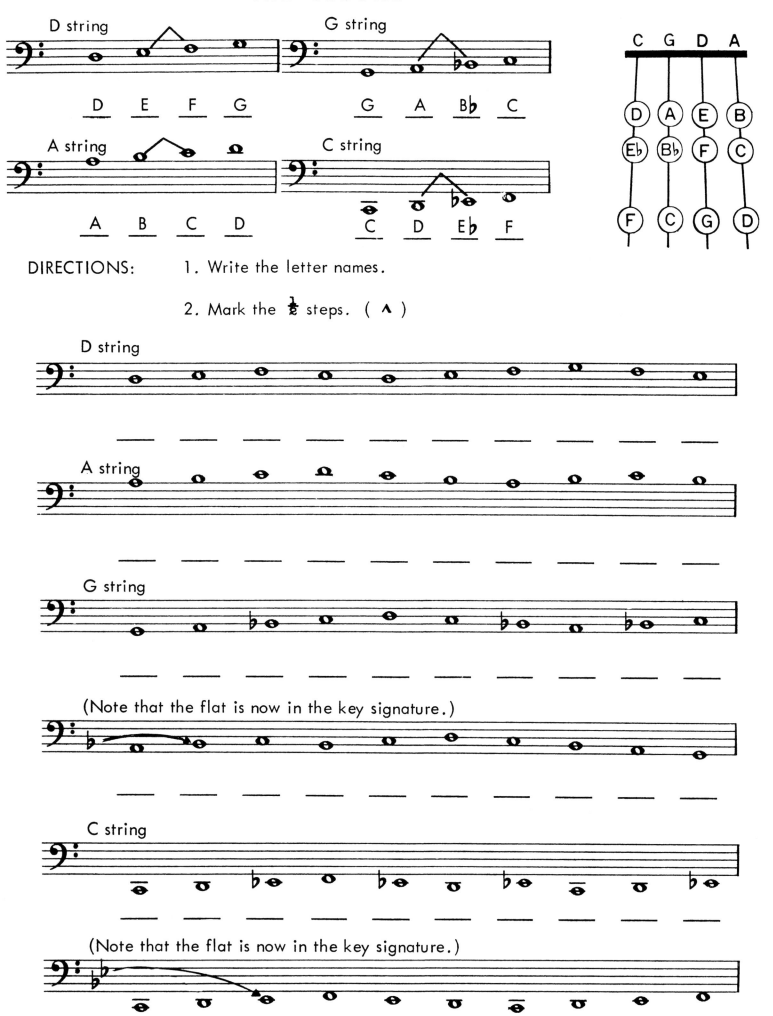

DIRECTIONS: 1. Write the letter names.

2. Mark the ½ steps. (∧)

THE 1-2 PATTERN

DIRECTIONS:

1. Write the notes that occur on each string if the ½ step occurs between the 1st and 2nd fingers. (Use accidentals.)

2. Name the notes.

3. Mark the ½ steps. (∧)

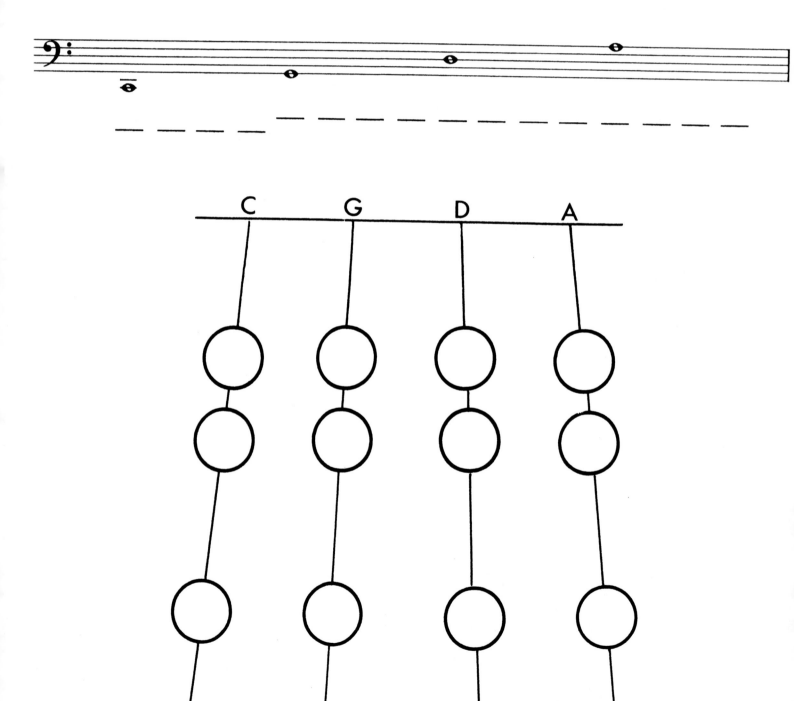

SECOND FINGERS

Key of G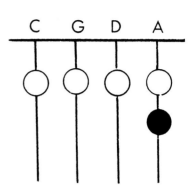

1. Name the second finger note: _____ .

2. C is second finger because there is no _____ in the key signature.

Key of C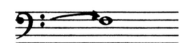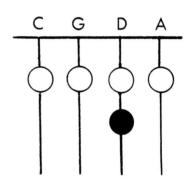

1. Name this second finger note: _____ .

2. F is second finger because there is no _____ in the key signature.

Key of F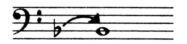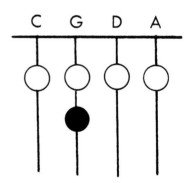

1. Name this second finger note: _____ .

2. B ♮ is second finger because _____ is in the key signature.

Key of B ♭

1. Name this second finger note: _____ .

2. E ♮ is second finger because _____ is in the key signature.

SECOND AND THIRD FINGERS

Key of D

On the C, we use 3rd because it is _____ _____ .

On the G, we use 3rd because it is _____ _____ .

On the D, we use 3rd because _____ is in the key signature.

On the A, we use 3rd because _____ is in the key signature.

Key of G

On the C, we use _____ finger because it is _____ _____ .

On the G, we use _____ finger because it is _____ _____ .

On the D, we use _____ finger because _____ is in the key signature.

On the A, we use _____ finger because it is _____ _____ .

Key of C

On the C, we use _____ finger because it is _____ _____ .

On the G, we use _____ finger because it is _____ _____ .

On the D, we use _____ finger because there is no _____ in the key signature.

On the A, we use _____ finger because there is no _____ in the key signature.

Key of F

On the C, we use _____ finger because it is _____ _____ .

On the G, we use _____ finger because _____ is in the key signature.

On the D, we use _____ finger because there is no _____ in the key signature.

On the A, we use _____ finger because there is no _____ in the key signature.

Key of B♭

On the C, we use _____ finger because _____ is in the key signature.

On the G, we use _____ finger because _____ is in the key signature.

On the D, we use _____ finger because there is no _____ in the key signature.

On the A, we use _____ finger because there is no _____ in the key signature.

QUIZ

Name the following keys and mark "2" or "3" opposite the second or third finger notes.

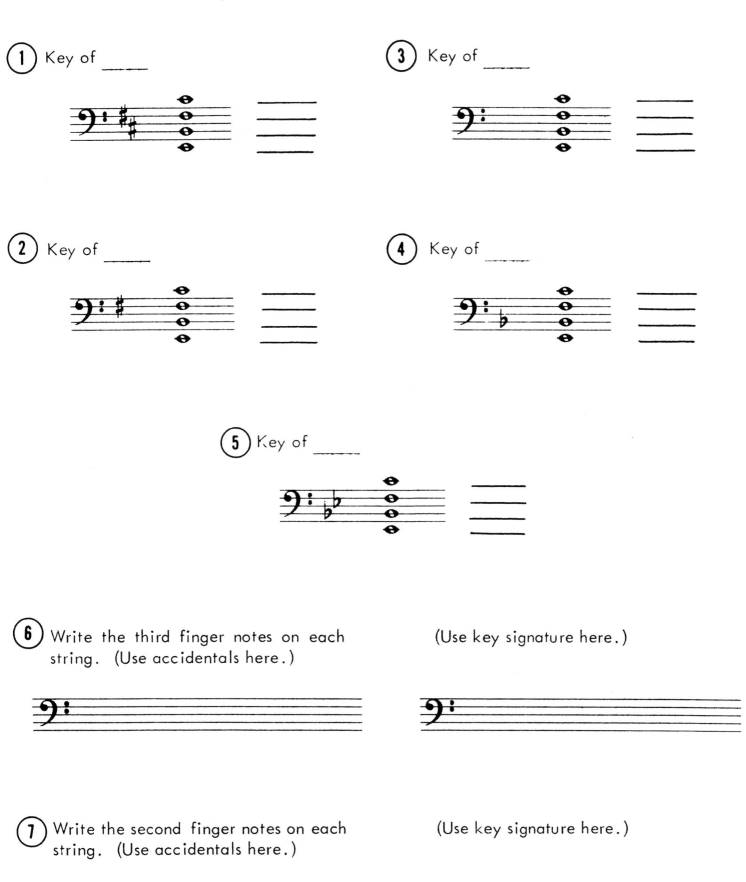

① Key of ____

② Key of ____

③ Key of ____

④ Key of ____

⑤ Key of ____

⑥ Write the third finger notes on each string. (Use accidentals here.)

(Use key signature here.)

⑦ Write the second finger notes on each string. (Use accidentals here.)

(Use key signature here.)

38

SCALES

DIRECTIONS:

1. Write in the names of the notes.

2. Write the names of the sharps or flats in the squares.

3. Mark the ½ steps. (∧)

Key of C

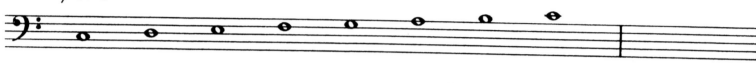

Key of G

Key of D

Key of F

MORE SCALES

DIRECTIONS:

1. Complete the scale.

2. Write in the names of the notes.

3. Mark the $\frac{1}{2}$ steps. (∧)

4. Write in the key signature.

Key of C

Key of G

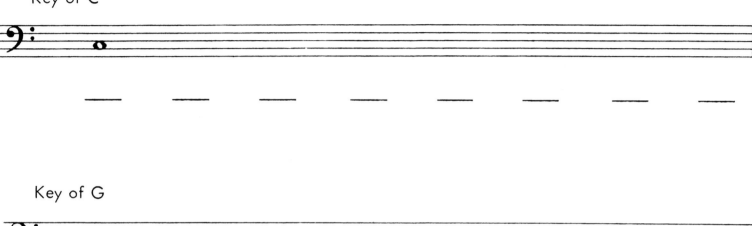

Key of D

Key of F

KEY PATTERN

DIRECTIONS:

1. Write the notes that occur in this key.
2. Mark the $\frac{1}{2}$ steps. (∧)
3. Name the notes.

This is the key of _____ .

The $\frac{1}{2}$ steps are _____ and _____, _____ and _____ .

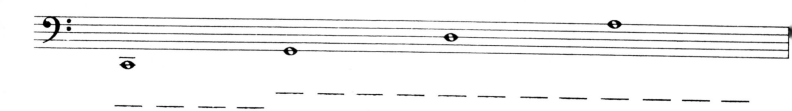

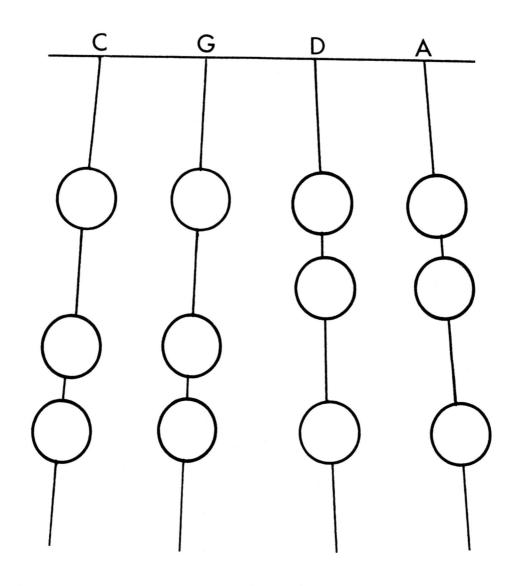

KEY PATTERN

DIRECTIONS:

1. Write the notes that occur in this key.
2. Mark the ½ steps. (⋀)
3. Name the notes.

This is the key of _____ .

The sharped note is _____ .

The ½ steps are _____ and _____ , _____ and _____ .

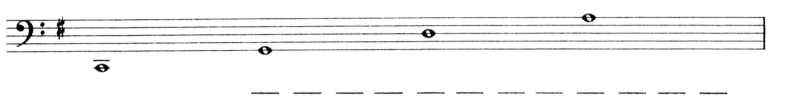

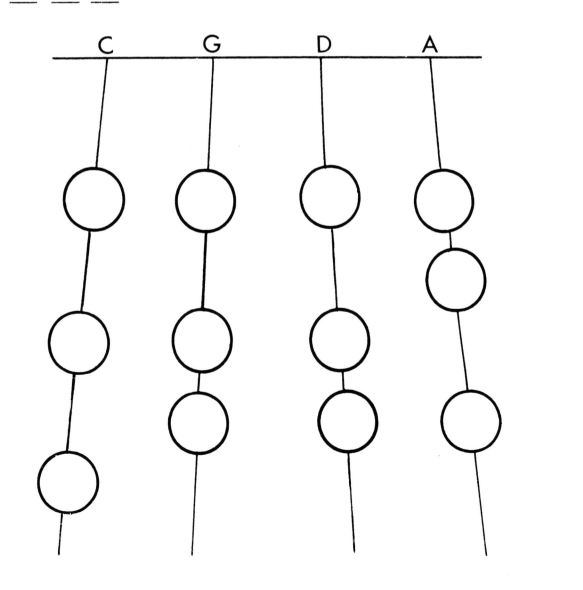

KEY PATTERN

DIRECTIONS:

1. Write the notes that occur in this key.
2. Mark the $\frac{1}{2}$ steps. (∧)
3. Name the notes.

This is the key of _____ .

The sharped notes are _____ and _____ .

The $\frac{1}{2}$ steps are _____ and _____ , _____ and _____ .

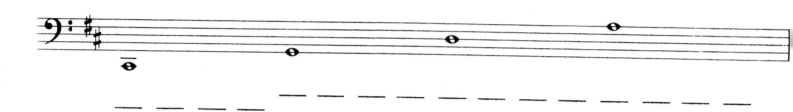

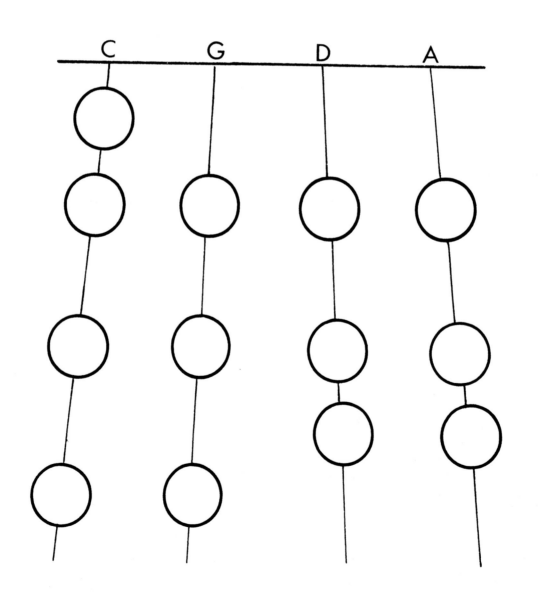

KEY PATTERN

DIRECTIONS:

1. Write the notes that occur in this key.
2. Mark the $\frac{1}{2}$ steps. (∧)
3. Name the notes.

This is the key of _____ .

The flatted note is _____ .

The $\frac{1}{2}$ steps are _____ and _____ , _____ and _____ .

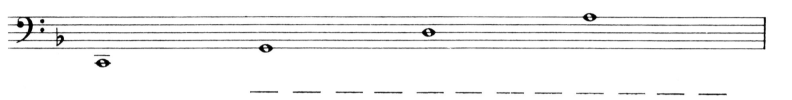

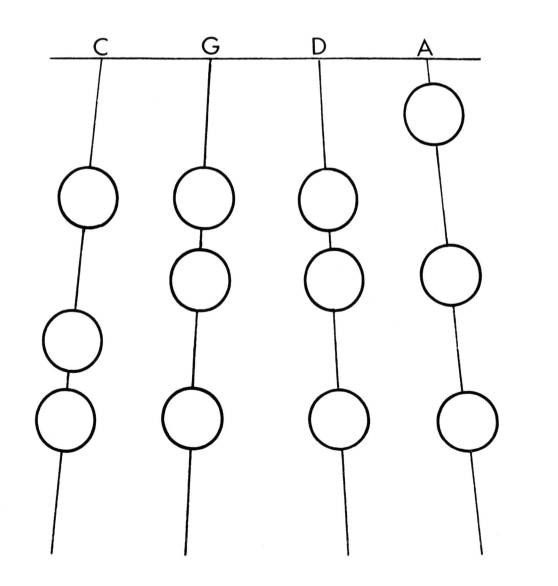

C   G   D   A

TEST

DIRECTIONS:

Write the letter names in the circles.

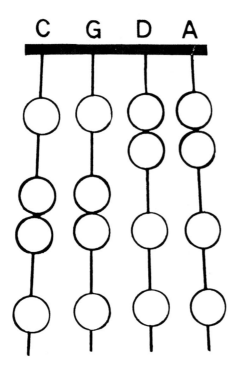

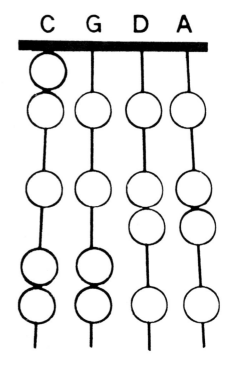

1. The above pattern is for the key of ____ .   3. The above pattern is for the key of ____ .

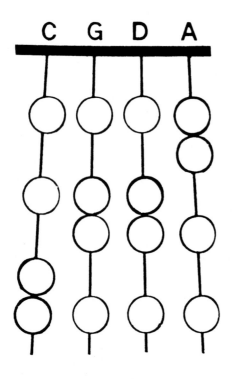

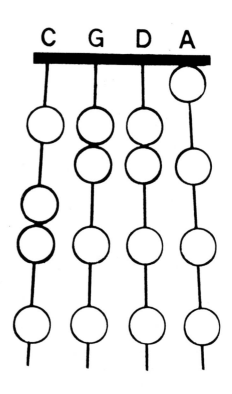

2. The above pattern is for the key of ____ .   4. The above pattern is for the key of ____ .

CONGRATULATIONS UPON THE COMPLETION OF BOOK I ! ! !

You are now ready for WORKBOOK FOR STRINGS, Book II, which covers all of the keys, terms, and signs that you must know to become a better orchestra member.